HOW TO ACHIEVE BILLIONAIRE STATUS AT A YOUNG AGE
BY
WILLIAM JONES
2023

How to Achieve Billionaire Status at a Young Age by William Jones
This edition was created and published by Mamba Press
©MambaPress 2023

Contents

Preface
    Chapter 1: Introduction: The Path to Extraordinary Wealth
    Chapter 2: Cultivating the Mindset of a Billionaire
    Chapter 3: Identifying Lucrative Opportunities
    Chapter 4: The Art of Networking and Relationship Building
    Chapter 5: Entrepreneurship: Building from the Ground Up
    Chapter 6: Mastering Financial Intelligence
    Chapter 7: Leveraging Technology and Innovation
    Chapter 8: The Importance of Resilience and Adaptability
    Chapter 9: Scaling Your Ventures to the Billion-Dollar Mark
    Chapter 10: Giving Back and Leaving a Lasting Legacy
    Chapter 11: Maintaining Work-Life Balance and Wellbeing
    Chapter 12: Case Studies of Young Billionaire Achievers
    Chapter 13: Looking Ahead: The Future of Young Billionaires
    Chapter 14: Conclusion
    Appendix: Resources and Tools for Aspiring Billionaires
    Appendix: Checklist for Young Billionaire Success

Preface

The journey to achieving billionaire status at a young age is a pursuit that requires a combination of vision, determination, innovation, and a commitment to personal growth. This book is a guide for those who aspire to reach extraordinary heights and redefine what is possible in the world of entrepreneurship and success.

In the pages that follow, you'll find a comprehensive exploration of the strategies, mindsets, and principles that have propelled young individuals to billionaire achievement. From cultivating the mindset of a billionaire and identifying lucrative opportunities to mastering financial intelligence, leveraging technology, and leaving a lasting legacy, each chapter offers insights, case studies, and actionable steps to guide you on your path.

Throughout this book, you'll discover the stories of young billionaire achievers who have left an indelible mark on industries, communities, and the world. Their journeys serve as both inspiration and a testament to the power of perseverance, innovation, and the pursuit of a grand vision.

While the road to young billionaire success is not without its challenges and setbacks, it is a journey that holds the promise of transformation, impact, and the fulfillment of audacious dreams. As you immerse yourself in the chapters that follow, I encourage you to approach this journey with an open mind, a hunger for knowledge, and an unwavering determination to reach your full potential.

Remember, becoming a young billionaire is not just about accumulating wealth; it's about embracing your potential as a change-maker, innovator, and leader. It's about using your resources, influence, and creativity to leave a lasting legacy that positively impacts the lives of others.

As you embark on this journey of growth, discovery, and achievement, may this book serve as a guiding light—one that empowers you to overcome obstacles, seize opportunities, and create a future that exceeds your wildest aspirations.

Here's to your pursuit of young billionaire success—a journey that begins with a single step and has the potential to transform not only your life but the lives of countless others.

Wishing you every success,
William Jones, 27-08-2023

Introduction: The Path to Extraordinary Wealth

In a world that's constantly evolving and presenting new opportunities, the allure of achieving billionaire status at a young age has captured the imagination of countless individuals. The idea of amassing enormous wealth, realizing dreams at an early stage of life, and making a significant impact on the world is undeniably appealing. This book, "How to Achieve Billionaire Status at a Young Age," is your guide to navigating this complex journey.

The Dream and the Reality

Aspiring to become a young billionaire is not just about money; it's a reflection of the desire to push boundaries, challenge the status quo, and create a legacy that resonates for generations to come. However, this dream is often romanticized and misconstrued. It's crucial to approach this journey with clear eyes and a realistic understanding of the challenges and sacrifices it entails.

Defying Convention

Historically, achieving billionaire status required decades of work and a lifetime of accumulation. But the digital age has rewritten the rules, allowing for accelerated success through technology, innovation, and unconventional thinking. Young entrepreneurs are leveraging their creativity, intelligence, and determination to disrupt industries, create new markets, and generate wealth at a pace that was once thought impossible.

The Roadmap Ahead

This book isn't a promise of overnight success or a shortcut to riches. It's a roadmap that merges timeless principles with cutting-edge strategies to help you set off on your journey toward young billionaire success. From cultivating the right mindset and identifying lucrative opportunities to mastering financial intelligence and maintaining work-life balance, each chapter is designed to provide you with actionable insights and practical steps.

Taking Ownership of Your Future

You hold the pen to write your story. The chapters ahead will provide you with the tools, knowledge, and inspiration to take charge of your future and craft a narrative that defies expectations. Whether you're a budding entrepreneur, a visionary with an idea, or someone eager to challenge themselves in pursuit of greatness, this book is for you.

As you embark on this adventure, remember that becoming a young billionaire is not just about the destination; it's about the transformation that occurs along the way. The journey will test your resilience, expand your horizons, and shape you into a leader capable of navigating uncharted waters.

So, are you ready to delve into the mindset, strategies, and principles that can propel you toward unlocking billionaire success at a young age? Let's begin the exploration and discovery together, with an open heart and a determined spirit. Your journey to extraordinary wealth and impact starts now.

Cultivating the Mindset of a Billionaire

In the quest for young billionaire success, the journey begins within. The mindset you cultivate becomes the foundation upon which your empire is built. The billionaires who have achieved remarkable success at a young age share a common trait: a resolute and unwavering belief in their abilities.

1. Embrace the Growth Mindset

At the core of the billionaire mindset is the concept of a growth mindset. This perspective sees challenges as opportunities for growth, setbacks as learning experiences, and effort as the path to mastery. A growth mindset frees you from the constraints of a fixed mentality and empowers you to continuously evolve.

2. Set Ambitious Goals

Billionaires don't merely set goals; they set audacious, seemingly impossible goals. These goals serve as beacons that guide their efforts and focus their energies. When you set extraordinary goals, you tap into hidden reservoirs of determination and creativity that propel you forward.

3. Embrace Risk and Failure

Risk-taking is an inherent part of the billionaire's journey. While calculated risks are taken, they understand that failure is a stepping stone to success. Each failure offers lessons that contribute to future victories. Embracing the possibility of failure allows you to push your boundaries and venture into uncharted territories.

4. Cultivate an Unshakable Self-Belief

Believe in your vision, your abilities, and your potential to achieve greatness. Self-doubt is a hindrance that stifles innovation and progress. Billionaires have an unshakeable self-belief that fuels their endeavors even in the face of skepticism or adversity.

5. Learn Continuously

The pursuit of knowledge is a hallmark of the billionaire mindset. Whether through formal education, self-study, or learning from experiences, they understand that staying curious and informed is essential. Learning not only enhances skills but also opens doors to novel opportunities.

6. Visualize Success

Visualization is a powerful tool used by billionaires to manifest their aspirations. By vividly imagining their success, they create a mental roadmap that guides their actions. Visualization aligns your subconscious mind with your conscious goals, making the path to achievement clearer.

7. Surround Yourself with Excellence

Your environment shapes your mindset. Surround yourself with individuals who inspire, challenge, and uplift you. Mentorship and collaboration expose you to diverse perspectives, accelerate your learning curve, and provide a support network during challenging times.

8. Practice Persistence and Patience

Billionaires understand that success rarely happens overnight. Persistence in the face of adversity and the ability to weather long-term challenges are paramount. Patience allows you to avoid premature pivots and remain committed to your vision.

9. Express Gratitude

Gratitude keeps the billionaire grounded amidst the pursuit of wealth. Acknowledge the progress you've made, the opportunities you've been given, and the people who've supported you. Gratitude fosters positivity and attracts more of the same into your life.

Cultivating the mindset of a billionaire isn't a one-time endeavor; it's a continuous process of growth, self-discovery, and refinement. Remember that your thoughts, beliefs, and attitudes shape your reality. As you internalize these principles, you're laying the groundwork for the success that lies ahead.

Identifying Lucrative Opportunities

In the world of young billionaire success, recognizing and seizing lucrative opportunities is a critical skill. Billionaires are adept at spotting trends, uncovering gaps in the market, and capitalizing on emerging industries. Their ability to identify opportunities sets them apart and propels them toward extraordinary wealth.

1. **Stay Vigilant for Trends**

Observing trends in technology, consumer behavior, and societal shifts is paramount. Keep a watchful eye on changes and disruptions happening around you. The early identification of trends can position you to create innovative solutions or enter untapped markets.

2. **Solve Pressing Problems**

Billionaires often begin their journeys by solving real problems faced by a large audience. Identifying pain points and designing solutions that alleviate them can lead to groundbreaking products or services. Addressing significant challenges can pave the way for substantial financial rewards.

3. **Explore Emerging Industries**

New industries are constantly emerging due to advancements in technology and shifts in societal needs. Being an early entrant into such industries can provide a competitive advantage. Research and analyze the potential of nascent sectors to determine where your skills and passions align.

4. **Leverage Your Unique Perspective**

Your individual experiences, passions, and expertise can lead you to opportunities others might overlook. Your distinct viewpoint might be the catalyst for a fresh perspective on an existing problem or a new approach to an industry.

5. **Understand Consumer Behavior**

Understanding what drives consumer decisions can reveal untapped niches and demand patterns. Analyze purchasing habits, preferences, and pain points to identify gaps in the market where you can introduce innovative solutions.

6. Think Global

In today's interconnected world, opportunities are not confined by geographical boundaries. Consider how your ideas or products can serve a global audience. Expanding your horizons can lead to exponential growth and impact.

7. Collaborate and Network

Engage with diverse individuals and industries to expand your insights. Collaborations and partnerships can open doors to opportunities you might not have encountered otherwise. Networking exposes you to new ideas, markets, and potential co-founders.

8. Predict Industry Disruptions

Industries are susceptible to disruptions that can reshape entire markets. Stay informed about technological advancements and societal shifts that could disrupt traditional models. Anticipating these changes allows you to pivot or innovate in response.

9. Evaluate Competition and White Spaces

Analyzing competitors can help you identify gaps or weaknesses in the market that you can exploit. Conversely, white spaces are areas that are underserved or ignored by existing players, presenting an opportunity for differentiation.

10. Stay Adaptable

Opportunities may present themselves unexpectedly. Be open to adjusting your plans and strategies to embrace new prospects as they arise. Flexibility and agility are key attributes of successful entrepreneurs.

Identifying lucrative opportunities requires a combination of curiosity, research, and a willingness to take calculated risks. By honing your ability to spot these openings and acting on them decisively, you're positioning yourself on the path to billionaire success.

The Art of Networking and Relationship Building

In the journey to young billionaire success, the value of networking and building meaningful relationships cannot be overstated. Billionaires recognize that their network is not just a collection of contacts; it's a web of opportunities, guidance, and support that propels them forward.

1. Cultivate Authentic Connections

Authenticity is the cornerstone of effective networking. Approach interactions with a genuine interest in getting to know others, rather than solely seeking what they can offer. Building authentic relationships fosters trust and mutual respect.

2. Diversify Your Network

Connect with individuals from diverse backgrounds, industries, and expertise areas. A well-rounded network exposes you to different perspectives, leading to innovative insights and opportunities that you might not encounter within your own bubble.

3. Leverage Digital Platforms

The digital age has revolutionized networking. Utilize social media platforms, professional networks, and online communities to connect with like-minded individuals and industry experts. Online presence can amplify your visibility and reach.

4. Attend Events and Conferences

Participate in conferences, workshops, and industry events. These gatherings provide fertile ground for networking, allowing you to meet potential collaborators, investors, and mentors face-to-face.

5. Seek Mentorship

Mentors are invaluable guides who offer wisdom and insights gained from their own experiences. Identify individuals whose accomplishments and values align with your goals, and don't hesitate to reach out for mentorship.

6. Give Before You Receive

Effective networking is a two-way street. Offer value to your connections before seeking favors or opportunities. Contributing your expertise, insights, or resources builds goodwill and reciprocity within your network.

7. Be a Connector

Introduce people within your network who could benefit from each other's expertise or resources. Being a connector not only strengthens your relationships but also positions you as a valuable hub within your industry.

8. Maintain Relationships

Building relationships is an ongoing process. Stay in touch with your connections, offer updates on your ventures, and show a genuine interest in their endeavors. Regular communication maintains the vibrancy of your network.

9. Leverage Serendipity

Chance encounters and unexpected connections can lead to remarkable opportunities. Keep an open mind and embrace the serendipity that often arises in networking situations.

10. Give Back to the Community

Contributing to your community through workshops, talks, or volunteer work establishes you as a thought leader and adds to your network. It's a way to showcase your expertise and create lasting connections.

11. Practice Active Listening

Listening attentively to others demonstrates respect and understanding. Active listening helps you grasp their needs, aspirations, and challenges, enabling you to offer relevant insights and support.

12. Exude Professionalism and Gratitude

Present yourself in a professional manner and express gratitude for the time and assistance your network provides. Professionalism and gratitude enhance your reputation and reinforce the positive image you project.

Networking is a lifelong skill that continuously evolves and evolves with you. The relationships you cultivate have the potential to fuel your journey to billionaire status by opening doors, providing guidance, and offering opportunities that propel you toward your goals.

Entrepreneurship: Building from the Ground Up

At the heart of young billionaire success lies the art of entrepreneurship. Billionaires are visionary leaders who transform ideas into thriving businesses. This chapter delves into the process of building a venture from scratch and navigating the challenging yet rewarding path of entrepreneurship.

1. Ideation and Concept Development

Innovation often begins with a single idea. Cultivate a culture of curiosity and creativity that encourages brainstorming and idea generation. Filter these ideas through the lens of market demand, feasibility, and personal passion.

2. Market Research and Validation

Thoroughly research your target market to understand its needs, preferences, and pain points. Validate your business concept through surveys, focus groups, or prototypes. Ensuring a market fit is crucial before moving forward.

3. Crafting a Business Plan

A well-structured business plan outlines your vision, mission, target market, competitive landscape, marketing strategy, operational plan, and financial projections. A comprehensive plan serves as a roadmap and attracts potential investors.

4. Funding Strategies

Billionaires understand that capital is the lifeblood of a business. Explore various funding options, such as bootstrapping, angel investors, venture capital, or crowdfunding. Each option has its own implications for ownership and control.

5. Product Development and Iteration

Create a prototype or minimum viable product (MVP) that allows you to gather feedback from potential customers. Iterate and refine your product based on this feedback to ensure it meets market expectations.

6. Building a Strong Team

Surround yourself with individuals who share your vision and bring diverse skills to the table. A cohesive team is vital for executing your business plan effectively and overcoming challenges together.

7. Effective Leadership

Billionaire entrepreneurs lead by example. They inspire their teams with a clear vision, effective communication, and a commitment to their company's values. Leadership that fosters trust and empowerment yields exceptional results.

8. Sales and Marketing Strategies

Develop a comprehensive sales and marketing strategy that reaches your target audience through various channels. Leverage digital platforms, content marketing, social media, and influencer partnerships to create brand awareness and drive sales.

9. Operational Efficiency

Efficient operations ensure that your business runs smoothly and optimally. Streamline processes, manage resources effectively, and implement technologies that enhance productivity and customer experience.

10. Adapting to Challenges

Entrepreneurship is rife with challenges, from market fluctuations to unexpected setbacks. Cultivate adaptability and resilience to navigate these hurdles. Learning from failures and pivoting when necessary are keys to long-term success.

11. Scaling for Growth

As your business gains traction, prepare for growth by scaling your operations. Expand your customer base, explore new markets, and consider partnerships or acquisitions that align with your business goals.

12. Ethical and Sustainable Practices

Billionaires recognize the importance of ethical business practices and social responsibility. Embrace sustainable practices, contribute positively to your community, and build a brand that prioritizes values alongside profits.

13. **Continuous Innovation**

Stay ahead of the curve by fostering a culture of innovation. Encourage your team to think creatively, explore new technologies, and anticipate future trends that can drive your business forward.

Entrepreneurship demands dedication, resilience, and a willingness to learn from every step of the journey. By mastering the art of building a business from the ground up, you're not only creating a vehicle for wealth generation but also contributing to the broader entrepreneurial landscape.

Mastering Financial Intelligence

In the pursuit of young billionaire success, mastering financial intelligence is paramount. Billionaires possess a deep understanding of money, investments, and wealth management. This chapter delves into the principles and strategies that underpin their financial acumen.

1. **Personal Finance Basics**

Billionaires begin by mastering their personal finances. Create a budget, manage expenses, and prioritize saving. Establishing a strong financial foundation is essential before venturing into wealth-building endeavors.

2. **Investment Fundamentals**

Understand different investment vehicles such as stocks, bonds, real estate, and alternative investments. Learn about risk and return trade-offs, diversification, and how to create a balanced investment portfolio.

3. **Risk Management Strategies**

Billionaires are not reckless; they mitigate risks through prudent strategies. Diversify investments to reduce exposure to any single asset or market. Consider hedging options and insurance to safeguard your financial interests.

4. **Leveraging Debt Strategically**

Debt can be a powerful tool if used wisely. Utilize leverage to invest in income-generating assets, but ensure that the returns outweigh the costs of borrowing.

5. **Understanding Taxes**

Taxes are a significant financial consideration. Educate yourself on tax laws and regulations to optimize your tax strategy. Seek professional advice to minimize your tax liabilities while staying compliant.

6. **Building Multiple Income Streams**

Billionaires rarely rely on a single source of income. Develop multiple income streams through investments, business ventures, royalties, and passive income sources. Diversification enhances financial stability.

7. Long-Term Wealth Creation

Think long-term when making financial decisions. Billionaires understand the power of compounding and prioritize investments that yield sustainable, steady growth over time.

8. Strategic Philanthropy

Philanthropy is a means of both giving back and optimizing your financial strategy. Structured philanthropy can yield tax benefits while making a positive impact on society.

9. Staying Informed

Stay updated on financial news, market trends, and economic indicators. Informed decisions are more likely to yield positive results, and a well-rounded understanding of the financial landscape enhances your decision-making.

10. Seeking Professional Guidance

Billionaires often consult financial advisors, tax experts, and wealth managers to optimize their financial strategies. These professionals offer specialized knowledge and can help you navigate complex financial scenarios.

11. Avoiding Emotional Decision-Making

Emotions can cloud judgment in financial matters. Develop discipline to avoid impulsive decisions during market fluctuations. Base your choices on well-reasoned analysis and long-term goals.

12. Measuring and Tracking Progress

Regularly assess your financial goals and track your progress. Adjust your strategies as circumstances change and stay focused on achieving your wealth-building objectives.

13. Ethical Financial Practices

Ethics and integrity are integral to financial success. Strive for transparency in your financial dealings, prioritize fair business practices, and give back to society responsibly.

Mastering financial intelligence is an ongoing journey that requires continuous learning, adaptability, and a commitment to making informed decisions. By developing a robust understanding of financial principles and strategies, you're equipping yourself to navigate the intricate world of wealth with confidence and competence.

Leveraging Technology and Innovation

In the realm of young billionaire success, technology and innovation are powerful catalysts that propel individuals to unprecedented heights. This chapter explores how billionaires harness the potential of technology to disrupt industries, create new opportunities, and drive exponential growth.

1. Embracing Technological Trends

Billionaires are at the forefront of adopting emerging technologies. Stay informed about trends such as artificial intelligence, blockchain, automation, and the Internet of Things. Recognize their potential to revolutionize industries.

2. Identifying Market Gaps

Technology often uncovers unmet needs and inefficiencies. Identify areas where technology can provide innovative solutions, streamline processes, or enhance customer experiences.

3. Developing Tech-Driven Solutions

Create products or services that leverage technology to address identified market gaps. Develop user-friendly interfaces, efficient processes, and seamless experiences that set you apart from competitors.

4. Disrupting Traditional Models

Billionaires disrupt traditional industries by introducing technology-driven alternatives. Airbnb disrupted the hospitality industry, and Uber transformed transportation. Identify industries ripe for disruption and create innovative solutions.

5. Investing in Research and Development

Invest resources in research and development to stay ahead of technological advancements. Develop proprietary technologies, enhance existing products, and position yourself as an industry leader.

6. Collaborating with Tech Experts

Forge partnerships with tech experts, software developers, and engineers. Collaborative efforts combine your industry expertise with their technical knowledge, resulting in groundbreaking solutions.

7. Scaling through Digital Platforms

Digital platforms enable global reach and rapid scaling. Leverage e-commerce, online marketplaces, and digital advertising to expand your customer base beyond geographical limitations.

8. Data-Driven Decision-Making

Data analytics provides valuable insights into customer behavior, market trends, and performance metrics. Utilize data to make informed decisions and refine your strategies.

9. Investing in Cybersecurity

With technological advancements come cybersecurity risks. Protect your business and customer data by investing in robust cybersecurity measures to maintain trust and avoid costly breaches.

10. Creating Exponential Value

Technology allows for exponential growth beyond linear limits. Consider how your products or services can create a network effect, where the value increases as more users participate.

11. Fostering a Culture of Innovation

Nurture a workplace culture that encourages innovation and creative thinking. Provide avenues for employees to share ideas, experiment, and contribute to the company's technological evolution.

12. Staying Adaptable to Change

Technology evolves rapidly. Stay adaptable and open to integrating new tools and platforms that enhance your business operations and keep you competitive.

Leveraging technology and innovation is more than adopting the latest gadgets; it's about embracing change, foreseeing possibilities, and pushing boundaries. By infusing your entrepreneurial endeavors with the transformative power of technology, you can redefine industries, create novel solutions, and position yourself as a leader in a rapidly evolving landscape.

The Importance of Resilience and Adaptability

In the journey toward young billionaire success, resilience and adaptability are essential traits that enable individuals to navigate challenges, setbacks, and ever-changing circumstances. This chapter delves into the critical role these attributes play in achieving extraordinary goals.

1. Embracing the Growth Mindset

Resilience begins with adopting a growth mindset. View challenges as opportunities for learning and growth rather than insurmountable obstacles. Embrace the belief that setbacks are stepping stones toward success.

2. Learning from Failure

Billionaires understand that failure is an inevitable part of any journey. Rather than fearing failure, extract valuable lessons from it. Analyze what went wrong, adjust your approach, and move forward with newfound insights.

3. Adapting to Market Shifts

Industries evolve, and market conditions change. Be prepared to adapt your strategies and offerings to align with shifting trends. Being agile allows you to seize new opportunities and overcome unexpected challenges.

4. Managing Uncertainty

Uncertainty is a constant in entrepreneurship. Develop strategies to manage risk and make informed decisions even in the face of ambiguity. Flexibility and adaptability enable you to pivot when necessary.

5. Building Emotional Resilience

Entrepreneurship can be emotionally taxing. Develop emotional intelligence to navigate stress, frustration, and setbacks. Practice mindfulness, self-care, and seek support when needed.

6. Seeking Feedback and Criticism

Constructive feedback is invaluable for growth. Welcome criticism as a means of improvement, and use it to refine your strategies and offerings. A willingness to learn from others demonstrates resilience.

7. **Maintaining a Long-Term Perspective**

Billionaires focus on the long term. A setback in the short term doesn't define your journey. Keep your eyes on your ultimate goals and remain committed to your vision.

8. **Turning Setbacks into Opportunities**

Resilient individuals find opportunities within challenges. Adversity can spark innovation and lead to new directions. The ability to transform setbacks into stepping stones sets you apart.

9. **Cultivating a Support Network**

Surround yourself with a support network of mentors, peers, and friends who uplift you during difficult times. A strong support system provides encouragement and perspective.

10. **Maintaining Consistency in Adversity**

Consistency is key, even when faced with challenges. Staying disciplined and committed to your goals during tough times accelerates your progress when conditions improve.

11. **Modeling Success Stories**

Study the experiences of successful entrepreneurs who overcame adversity. Their stories serve as inspiration and remind you that setbacks are a natural part of the journey.

12. **Continuing to Innovate**

Resilience and adaptability go hand in hand with innovation. Use setbacks as opportunities to innovate and improve your offerings, processes, and strategies.

Resilience and adaptability are the bedrock of young billionaire success. They empower you to persevere through setbacks, seize opportunities, and evolve with changing circumstances. By cultivating these qualities, you're equipped to thrive in the dynamic world of entrepreneurship and achieve remarkable outcomes.

Scaling Your Ventures to the Billion-Dollar Mark

For those pursuing young billionaire success, scaling ventures to the billion-dollar mark is the pinnacle of achievement. This chapter explores the strategies, mindset, and actions required to take your business from its early stages to a global powerhouse.

1. **Setting Ambitious Growth Goals**

Scaling requires audacious goals. Define clear, measurable objectives that reflect your ambition to grow exponentially. Align your team's efforts toward achieving these milestones.

2. **Optimizing Operations for Scale**

Efficient operations are crucial for scaling. Streamline processes, invest in technology, and create systems that can handle increased demand without sacrificing quality.

3. **Leveraging Technology for Efficiency**

Technology accelerates scaling by automating tasks, enhancing communication, and improving customer experiences. Integrate scalable tech solutions that support your growth trajectory.

4. **Expanding Market Reach**

Scaling necessitates expanding your market reach. Identify new geographic markets or customer segments that align with your products or services. Tailor your strategies to resonate with diverse audiences.

5. **Building a High-Performance Team**

A scalable business requires a skilled, cohesive team. Attract top talent, provide ongoing training, and foster a culture of excellence that drives innovation and growth.

6. **Developing Strategic Partnerships**

Collaborate with strategic partners to leverage their expertise, resources, and customer base. Partnerships can accelerate growth by providing access to new markets and complementary offerings.

7. Investing in Marketing and Branding

Invest in marketing campaigns that amplify your brand's visibility and reach. Develop a strong brand identity and narrative that resonates with your target audience.

8. Securing Funding for Expansion

Scaling requires capital. Explore funding options such as venture capital, private equity, or strategic investors. Choose partners who share your vision and can provide not just funds, but also guidance.

9. Measuring and Analyzing Performance

Track key performance indicators (KPIs) to gauge the effectiveness of your scaling strategies. Regularly review data and adjust your approach to optimize outcomes.

10. Maintaining Customer-Centricity

As you scale, prioritize maintaining a customer-centric approach. Ensuring customer satisfaction and addressing their evolving needs fosters loyalty and positive word-of-mouth.

11. Addressing Growing Pains

Scaling comes with challenges. Anticipate issues like increased demand, operational complexity, and potential dilution of company culture. Develop strategies to mitigate these growing pains.

12. Staying Innovative and Nimble

While scaling, innovation remains critical. Encourage a culture of experimentation and creativity to continually introduce new products, features, or services that drive growth.

13. Leading with Vision

As a leader, your vision guides the scaling process. Communicate your goals, empower your team, and foster alignment to create a collective drive toward the billion-dollar mark.

Scaling to a billion-dollar enterprise requires strategic foresight, calculated risk-taking, and the ability to adapt to an ever-evolving landscape. By applying these principles and methodologies, you position your venture to achieve monumental success on a global stage.

Giving Back and Leaving a Lasting Legacy

In the pursuit of young billionaire success, the notion of giving back and leaving a meaningful legacy holds profound significance. This chapter explores how billionaires use their resources, influence, and platforms to create positive social impact and establish enduring legacies.

1. **Recognizing the Responsibility**

Billionaires acknowledge the ethical responsibility to contribute to the betterment of society. Embrace the concept that success carries an obligation to give back and make a difference.

2. **Strategic Philanthropy**

Approach philanthropy strategically. Identify causes that align with your values and business focus. Develop philanthropic initiatives that leverage your resources and expertise to address societal challenges.

3. **Creating Sustainable Initiatives**

Sustainable impact requires long-term commitment. Create initiatives that go beyond short-term fixes, aiming to create lasting change and address root causes of issues.

4. **Investing in Education**

Education is a powerful tool for empowerment. Establish educational programs, scholarships, or institutions that provide opportunities for underserved communities to access quality education.

5. **Supporting Entrepreneurship**

Promote economic empowerment by supporting entrepreneurship in underrepresented communities. Provide mentorship, resources, and funding to budding entrepreneurs.

6. **Environmental Conservation**

Consider the environmental impact of your business and explore ways to contribute to conservation efforts. Implement eco-friendly practices and support initiatives that protect the planet.

7. **Healthcare and Wellbeing**

Invest in healthcare initiatives that improve access to medical services and promote wellbeing. Address healthcare disparities and contribute to advancements in medical research.

8. Catalyzing Social Change

Billionaires have the platform to drive social change. Use your influence to raise awareness, influence policy, and advocate for social justice issues that align with your values.

9. Collaboration for Impact

Collaborate with other philanthropists, nonprofits, and organizations to amplify your impact. Collective efforts often achieve greater results than individual initiatives.

10. Transparency and Accountability

Transparency builds trust with stakeholders. Communicate your philanthropic efforts, share progress, and ensure resources are used efficiently to maximize impact.

11. Inspiring Others to Give Back

Lead by example and inspire others in your industry to embrace philanthropy. Your actions can spark a movement of positive change within your network and beyond.

12. Crafting a Legacy Beyond Wealth

Your legacy is more than financial success. Focus on the values, principles, and positive impact you leave behind. Consider how your business and philanthropic endeavors contribute to a better world.

13. Continuing to Learn and Adapt

Philanthropy is a continuous learning journey. Stay informed about evolving societal needs and adapt your initiatives to remain relevant and effective.

By channeling your success toward giving back, you're not only leaving a lasting impact on individuals and communities but also shaping a legacy that extends far beyond your lifetime. This commitment to social good enriches your journey toward young billionaire success and contributes to a world that benefits from your achievements.

Maintaining Work-Life Balance and Wellbeing

In the pursuit of young billionaire success, maintaining work-life balance and prioritizing personal wellbeing are essential components. This chapter delves into the importance of self-care, managing stress, and fostering a harmonious equilibrium between your professional and personal lives.

1. **Recognizing the Value of Balance**

Billionaires understand that success extends beyond financial achievements. Recognize that a balanced life encompasses health, relationships, personal growth, and professional accomplishments.

2. **Setting Boundaries**

Establish clear boundaries between work and personal life. Designate specific times for work, leisure, and family to prevent burnout and maintain a sense of control.

3. **Prioritizing Self-Care**

Self-care is non-negotiable. Regularly engage in activities that rejuvenate your mind, body, and spirit. Exercise, meditation, hobbies, and quality sleep contribute to overall wellbeing.

4. **Effective Time Management**

Efficient time management allows you to accomplish tasks while reserving time for personal pursuits. Prioritize tasks, delegate where possible, and optimize your workflow.

5. **Delegating Responsibilities**

Delegation is key to avoiding overwhelm. Empower your team to handle tasks, enabling you to focus on strategic decisions and activities that align with your strengths.

6. **Embracing the Power of No**

Saying no is essential to protect your time and energy. Politely decline commitments or projects that do not align with your priorities or contribute positively to your life.

7. Nurturing Relationships

Invest time in nurturing relationships with family and friends. Meaningful connections provide emotional support and enhance your overall sense of happiness.

8. Mindfulness and Stress Management

Practice mindfulness techniques to manage stress. Mindful breathing, meditation, and grounding exercises help reduce anxiety and enhance mental clarity.

9. Balancing Physical Health

Prioritize your physical health with regular exercise and a balanced diet. Physical wellbeing is foundational for sustained energy and mental acuity.

10. Unplugging from Technology

Disconnect from technology periodically to recharge. Engaging in screen-free activities allows you to be present in the moment and reduce digital fatigue.

11. Investing in Personal Growth

Allocate time for personal development. Read, learn, attend workshops, and engage in activities that contribute to your growth as an individual.

12. Seeking Professional Support

If stress or mental health challenges arise, seek support from professionals. Counseling, therapy, or coaching can provide valuable tools to navigate challenges.

13. Reflecting on Progress

Regularly assess your work-life balance and wellbeing. Reflect on whether your current lifestyle aligns with your values and goals, and make adjustments as needed.

A life of young billionaire success is most fulfilling when it encompasses both professional achievements and personal wellbeing. By maintaining work-life balance and prioritizing your health, relationships, and personal growth, you create a foundation for sustained happiness and success that extends far beyond financial accomplishments.

Case Studies of Young Billionaire Achievers

In this chapter, we'll delve into the inspiring stories of young individuals who achieved billionaire status through innovation, determination, and a unique blend of skills. These case studies highlight their journeys, strategies, and lessons that propelled them to extraordinary success.

1. Mark Zuckerberg: Redefining Social Connectivity

Mark Zuckerberg's journey from creating "The Facebook" in his college dorm room to leading one of the world's largest social media platforms is a testament to his innovative thinking. By recognizing the need for online social interaction, he revolutionized communication and connected billions of people globally. His relentless focus on user experience, adaptability to market changes, and commitment to privacy shaped Facebook's evolution into a tech giant.

2. Kylie Jenner: Building a Cosmetics Empire

Kylie Jenner leveraged her celebrity status and social media influence to create Kylie Cosmetics, a makeup brand that disrupted the beauty industry. By directly engaging with her fan base, capitalizing on trends, and maintaining authenticity, she amassed a loyal customer following. Jenner's ability to pivot and adapt her business strategy in response to market demands played a significant role in propelling her to billionaire status at a young age.

3. Brian Chesky: Transforming Hospitality with Airbnb

Brian Chesky co-founded Airbnb, an online marketplace that disrupted the traditional hospitality industry. By identifying a market gap and leveraging the power of the sharing economy, Chesky created a platform that allowed people to rent out their homes to travelers. His focus on user experience, design, and community building contributed to Airbnb's rapid growth and valuation in the billions.

4. Evan Spiegel and Bobby Murphy: Reinventing Communication with Snapchat

Evan Spiegel and Bobby Murphy introduced Snapchat, a multimedia messaging app that resonated with younger users seeking a more spontaneous and ephemeral way to communicate. By capitalizing on the visual nature of communication and continuously innovating features, they created a unique platform that captured the attention of a vast user base. Their ability to adapt to changing trends and refine the user experience contributed to Snapchat's success.

5. Elizabeth Holmes: Learning from the Downfall

Elizabeth Holmes founded Theranos with the ambition to revolutionize medical testing. However, her journey serves as a cautionary tale of the consequences of unethical practices and misrepresentation. While initially hailed as a young billionaire achiever, Holmes's actions led to legal challenges and the downfall of her company. Her story highlights the importance of integrity, transparency, and ethical decision-making in the pursuit of success.

These case studies underscore the diverse paths young billionaires take to achieve remarkable success. Whether through innovative tech solutions, disruptive business models, or social media influence, these individuals demonstrate the power of creativity, determination, adaptability, and ethical considerations on the road to becoming young billionaire achievers.

Looking Ahead: The Future of Young Billionaires

As we peer into the future, the landscape of young billionaire achievement is poised for evolution and transformation. This chapter explores the trends, challenges, and opportunities that will shape the journeys of aspiring young billionaires in the years to come.

1. Technological Innovation Continues

The pace of technological advancement shows no signs of slowing down. Young billionaires of the future will harness emerging technologies such as artificial intelligence, quantum computing, and biotechnology to create innovative solutions that disrupt industries and drive growth.

2. Impactful Sustainability Initiatives

Future young billionaires will be increasingly conscious of the planet's wellbeing. Sustainability will be a core focus, with ventures designed to address environmental challenges, reduce carbon footprints, and contribute to a more sustainable future.

3. Diverse and Inclusive Entrepreneurship

The entrepreneurial landscape will become more inclusive, welcoming individuals from diverse backgrounds and perspectives. The future will see young billionaires advocating for equality, social justice, and empowerment through their ventures.

4. Evolving Work Models

The concept of work and employment will transform with the rise of remote work, gig economy platforms, and flexible arrangements. Young billionaires will shape the future of work by creating platforms and initiatives that support this changing landscape.

5. Global Collaboration and Cross-Border Ventures

Digital connectivity will enable young billionaires to collaborate across geographical boundaries. Global partnerships and ventures will be the norm, creating a seamless flow of ideas, talent, and resources.

6. Personalized Health and Wellness

Advancements in healthcare and personalized wellness will be a focus for future young billionaires. Ventures will emerge to cater to individualized health needs, mental wellbeing, and preventive care.

7. Ethics and Transparency as Cornerstones

Ethics and transparency will remain vital as societal expectations rise. Future young billionaires will prioritize responsible business practices, authenticity, and social impact as integral components of their success.

8. Continuous Learning and Adaptability

The pace of change demands constant learning and adaptation. Future young billionaires will embrace a lifelong commitment to growth, regularly acquiring new skills and knowledge to stay relevant.

9. Resilience in the Face of Uncertainty

Navigating a volatile world, future young billionaires will possess heightened resilience and crisis management skills. The ability to pivot, innovate, and remain steadfast during challenging times will define their success.

10. Cultivating Human-Centered Technology

While technology will play a central role, future young billionaires will emphasize human-centric design. Ventures will prioritize enhancing the human experience, creating solutions that enrich lives and foster meaningful connections.

The future of young billionaire success is a dynamic landscape shaped by technological advancement, social consciousness, and an unwavering commitment to positive change. By staying attuned to these trends and maintaining a mindset of innovation, adaptability, and ethical responsibility, aspiring young billionaires can position themselves to thrive in the ever-evolving world of entrepreneurship.

Conclusion

The journey to young billionaire success is a remarkable path that requires a unique blend of passion, determination, innovation, and strategic thinking. Throughout this book, we've explored the diverse facets that contribute to achieving billionaire status at a young age. From cultivating the mindset of a billionaire and identifying lucrative opportunities to mastering financial intelligence, leveraging technology, and leaving a lasting legacy, each chapter has provided insights and strategies to guide you on your journey.

Becoming a young billionaire is not just about financial wealth; it's about creating a positive impact, contributing to society, and leaving a legacy that transcends generations. It's about pursuing your passion, embracing challenges, and continuously striving for excellence. It's about maintaining a work-life balance, prioritizing personal wellbeing, and valuing the relationships that enrich your life.

As you embark on your path to young billionaire success, remember that your journey is unique, and your story will be shaped by your individual experiences, choices, and aspirations. Embrace the lessons shared in this book, but also remain open to the unexpected opportunities and challenges that will undoubtedly arise along the way.

The future holds limitless possibilities for those who dare to dream big, work tirelessly, and remain committed to their vision. Whether you're driven by the desire to innovate, make a difference, or create a legacy, know that the pursuit of young billionaire success is a noble endeavor that has the potential to inspire, transform, and elevate not only your life but also the lives of countless others.

As you continue on your journey, may you find fulfillment, purpose, and success beyond measure. May you leave an indelible mark on the world and serve as an inspiration to those who follow in your footsteps. With the right mindset, strategies, and unwavering determination, you have the power to achieve the extraordinary and redefine what is possible in the world of entrepreneurship and beyond.

Here's to your journey of young billionaire success—a journey that knows no limits and is bound only by the depths of your imagination and the extent of your determination.

Appendix: Resources and Tools for Aspiring Billionaires

Achieving young billionaire success requires a combination of knowledge, skills, and access to valuable resources. In this appendix, you'll find a curated list of resources and tools to support your journey toward becoming a young billionaire.

1. **Books for Personal Development and Entrepreneurship:**

   - "Think and Grow Rich" by Napoleon Hill
   - "The Lean Startup" by Eric Ries
   - "Zero to One" by Peter Thiel
   - "The 4-Hour Workweek" by Timothy Ferriss
   - "Mindset: The New Psychology of Success" by Carol S. Dweck

2. **Online Learning Platforms:**

   - Coursera (www.coursera.org[1])
   - Udemy (www.udemy.com[2])
   - LinkedIn Learning (www.linkedin.com/learning[3])

3. **Financial Education and Investment Platforms:**

   - Investopedia (www.investopedia.com[4])
   - Robinhood (www.robinhood.com[5])
   - E*TRADE (www.etrade.com[6])

---

1. http://www.coursera.org/
2. http://www.udemy.com/
3. http://www.linkedin.com/learning
4. http://www.investopedia.com/
5. http://www.robinhood.com/
6. http://www.etrade.com/

4. **Networking and Professional Development:**

   - LinkedIn (www.linkedin.com[7])
   - Meetup (www.meetup.com[8])
   - Toastmasters International (www.toastmasters.org[9])

5. **Entrepreneurial Communities and Forums:**

   - Reddit Entrepreneur (www.reddit.com/r/Entrepreneur[10])
   - Indie Hackers (www.indiehackers.com[11])
   - StartupNation (www.startupnation.com[12])

6. **Business Tools and Software:**

   - Microsoft Office Suite (www.microsoft.com[13])
   - Google Workspace (workspace.google.com)
   - Trello (www.trello.com[14]) for project management
   - Canva (www.canva.com[15]) for graphic design

7. **Mentorship and Coaching Platforms:**

   - SCORE (www.score.org[16])
   - Clarity.fm (www.clarity.fm[17])

---

7. http://www.linkedin.com/

8. http://www.meetup.com/

9. http://www.toastmasters.org/

10. http://www.reddit.com/r/Entrepreneur

11. http://www.indiehackers.com/

12. http://www.startupnation.com/

13. http://www.microsoft.com/

14. http://www.trello.com/

15. http://www.canva.com/

16. http://www.score.org/

- Bravely (www.bravely.com[18])

8. Crowdfunding and Investment Platforms:

- Kickstarter (www.kickstarter.com[19])
- AngelList (www.angel.co[20])

9. Financial and Investment News:

- Bloomberg (www.bloomberg.com[21])
- CNBC (www.cnbc.com[22])
- Financial Times (www.ft.com[23])

10. Health and Wellness Apps:

- Calm (www.calm.com[24]) for meditation and relaxation
- MyFitnessPal (www.myfitnesspal.com[25]) for tracking health goals

11. Time Management and Productivity Tools:

- Todoist (www.todoist.com[26])
- RescueTime (www.rescuetime.com[27])

---

17. http://www.clarity.fm/
18. http://www.bravely.com/
19. http://www.kickstarter.com/
20. http://www.angel.co/
21. http://www.bloomberg.com/
22. http://www.cnbc.com/
23. http://www.ft.com/
24. http://www.calm.com/
25. http://www.myfitnesspal.com/
26. http://www.todoist.com/

Remember, these resources are meant to complement your journey and provide you with valuable knowledge, tools, and support. Tailor your use of these resources based on your individual goals, preferences, and needs. As you continue to learn, grow, and navigate the path to young billionaire success, these resources can serve as valuable companions on your remarkable journey.

---

27. http://www.rescuetime.com/

Appendix: Checklist for Young Billionaire Success

Achieving young billionaire success requires careful planning, strategic thinking, and consistent effort. Use this checklist as a reference to ensure you're on track to reach your goals.

1. Mindset and Personal Development:

- ☐ Cultivate a growth mindset that embraces challenges and learning opportunities.
- ☐ Continuously seek personal development through reading, courses, and self-reflection.
- ☐ Set clear and audacious goals for your journey to billionaire success.

2. Identifying Opportunities:

- ☐ Stay informed about market trends, emerging industries, and untapped opportunities.
- ☐ Identify gaps in existing markets and niches where you can provide innovative solutions.

3. Building Relationships and Networking:

- ☐ Cultivate a strong network of mentors, peers, and industry experts.
- ☐ Attend networking events, conferences, and workshops to expand your connections.

HOW TO ACHIEVE BILLIONAIRE STATUS AT A YOUNG AGE

4. Entrepreneurship and Innovation:

- ☐ Develop a unique value proposition for your business venture.
- ☐ Continuously innovate and adapt your products or services to meet changing demands.

5. Financial Intelligence:

- ☐ Educate yourself about personal finance, investments, and wealth management.
- ☐ Develop a diversified investment portfolio that aligns with your financial goals.

6. Technology and Innovation:

- ☐ Stay updated on technological trends and their potential impact on your industry.
- ☐ Explore ways to leverage technology to create innovative solutions.

7. Resilience and Adaptability:

- ☐ Embrace failure as a learning opportunity and use setbacks to fuel your growth.
- ☐ Develop resilience and the ability to adapt to changing circumstances.

8. Work-Life Balance and Wellbeing:

- ☐ Prioritize self-care, including exercise, mindfulness, and healthy habits.
- ☐ Set boundaries between work and personal life to avoid burnout.

9. Leaving a Legacy and Giving Back:

- ☐ Consider how you can use your success to make a positive impact on society.
- ☐ Engage in philanthropic initiatives and contribute to causes that align with your values.

10. Continuous Learning and Improvement:

- ☐ Stay curious and committed to lifelong learning.
- ☐ Regularly assess your progress and adjust your strategies as needed.

11. Ethical Decision-Making:

- ☐ Prioritize ethical business practices and transparency in all your endeavors.
- ☐ Make decisions that align with your values and contribute positively to society.

12. Setting Long-Term Goals:

- ☐ Define your long-term vision and the legacy you want to leave behind.

HOW TO ACHIEVE BILLIONAIRE STATUS AT A YOUNG AGE

- ☐ Develop a roadmap to achieve your billion-dollar goals step by step.

As you navigate your journey toward young billionaire success, use this checklist as a guide to ensure you're addressing key areas and staying focused on your goals. Remember that success is a continuous journey, and your dedication, innovation, and positive impact will shape not only your path but also the future of entrepreneurship.

www.ingramcontent.com/pod-product-compliance
Lightning Source LLC
LaVergne TN
LVHW041640070526
838199LV00052B/3469